AN EXAMINATION GUIDE
for
NURSERY NURSES
Volume 2

Jean Brain, Cert. Ed.
Molly D. Martin, R.G.N., H.V. Cert.

Stanley Thornes & Hulton

By the same authors:

CHILD CARE AND HEALTH
FOR NURSERY NURSES

AN EXAMINATION GUIDE
FOR NURSERY NURSES
Volume I

Published by Hulton

© *Jean Brain and Molly D. Martin* 1987

First published in Great Britain 1987 by
Stanley Thornes & Hulton
Old Station Drive
Leckhampton
Cheltenham GL53 0DN

British Library Cataloguing in Publication Data

Brain, Jean
  An examination guide for nursery nurses.
  Vol. 2
  1. Child rearing   2. Day care centres
  I. Title   II. Martin, Molly D.
  649'.1   HQ769

  ISBN 0 85950 717 3

Phototypeset in 10/11pt Linotron Palatino
by KEYTEC, Bridport, Dorset
Printed in Great Britain at The Bath Press, Avon

CONTENTS

INTRODUCTION

This is the second guide that we have produced to help nursery nurses pass their examination. In our first book, we discussed at some length the preparation for the examination. For this reason we do not propose to repeat here something which, after all, does not change. We should, however, like to include the following two suggestions passed on to us, which concern the planning of your essay answers.

1. It may make it easier to decide on headings if you ring the 'key' words, (thus), on the question paper. This may also serve as a visual reminder of the main track you should be keeping to, as you later ponder over how to express a point.

2. An alternative way of making a plan is to draw a web diagram. It can be quicker, and again, a visual reminder. For example, the reasons why a baby cries can be shown like this:

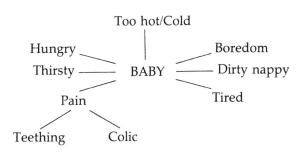

Look at the marks allocated for each part of the question to find out what the examiner considers the most important.

In response to requests, we have this time included a plan of *all* the answers to the essays, although still answering in full only the required number.

Finally, it remains for us to say, once again, 'Good luck in your examinations.'

EXAMPLE 1 OF A MULTIPLE CHOICE PAPER

1. A baby of nine months is expected to be able to:

    (a) walk alone
    (b) say six words with meaning
    (c) sit steadily on the floor
    (d) feed himself or herself with a spoon

2. 'Centile' charts are used to:

    (a) record a child's development
    (b) record a child's height and weight
    (c) record the amount a child eats
    (d) record the amount of liquid he or she drinks

3. A child is expected to walk unaided at:

    (a) ten months
    (b) twelve months
    (c) eighteen months
    (d) two years

4. Which would be the most suitable present for a four-year-old?

    (a) a jigsaw puzzle
    (b) a cardboard box
    (c) a teenaged doll
    (d) a Monopoly game

5. What is the Denver test?

    (a) a test of a newborn's condition
    (b) a test for phenylketonuria
    (c) a test of a baby's development
    (d) a test for diagnosis of dislocated hips

6. An antenatal mother's blood test shows an excessive amount of alphafeta protein. This could mean that:

    (a) the mother is anaemic
    (b) the baby has spina bifida
    (c) the mother has high blood pressure
    (d) the baby has Down's Syndrome

7.   Which is the least effective method of contraception?

(a) IUD
(b) the sheath
(c) the rhythm method
(d) the pill

8.   How can you prevent a sick child inhaling his vomit and suffocating?

(a) Put him in the recovery position.
(b) Get him to lie back quietly.
(c) Do not allow him a pillow.
(d) Let him take up his own position.

9.   At what age is a child approximately half her adult height?

(a) three years
(b) five years
(c) one and a half years
(d) two years

10.   The most suitable clothing for a six-week-old baby during a heat wave is:

(a) nappy and vest
(b) nappy and cotton dress
(c) nappy only
(d) nappy and 'Babygro'

11.   Footwear that is too tight is dangerous for a baby because it:

(a) can cause foot deformities
(b) can make the feet ache
(c) can cause chilblains
(d) will prevent the feet staying warm

12.   We sterilise bottles to:

(a) kill all germs
(b) prevent gastro-enteritis
(c) ensure that milk tastes good
(d) keep the bottle looking nice

13.   Which of the following can be classified as 'junk' food?

(a) crisps
(b) ice-cream
(c) chocolate
(d) 'instant' noodles

14. Which additive to food is thought to cause hyperactivity?

    (a) vitamins
    (b) yellow colouring
    (c) glucose
    (d) lemon flavouring

15. Which disease starts with runny nose and eyes?

    (a) measles
    (b) mumps
    (c) whooping cough
    (d) chicken-pox

16. Asthma, eczema and hay fever all belong to which of the following groups of diseases?

    (a) deficiency diseases
    (b) infectious diseases
    (c) allergic reactions
    (d) skin diseases

17. Which disease has been eradicated from the world?

    (a) smallpox
    (b) malaria
    (c) sandfly fever
    (d) typhus

18. Which of the following actions is most valuable in preventing dental decay?

    (a) eating an apple after meals
    (b) rinsing with water after meals
    (c) cleaning teeth thoroughly once a day
    (d) eating nothing in between meals

19. A five-year-old child is always scratching his bottom. The most likely explanation is that:

    (a) he is masturbating
    (b) he has threadworms
    (c) he needs a bath
    (d) he needs clean pants

20. All but one of the following groups of children are known to be particularly prone to hearing loss. Which is it?

    (a) Down's Syndrome children
    (b) twins
    (c) children in their first year at nursery/infant school
    (d) children with cerebral palsy

21. She sits on the beach. She bangs at the sand with the palm of her hand, puts some in her mouth. When handed a spade, she jabs randomly at the sand, holding the spade loosely at the top, and making little impression on the sand. This little girl is approximately:

    (a) six months old
    (b) one year old
    (c) three years old
    (d) four years old

22. Many sand-castles made by children under approximately three years do not turn out very well. This is chiefly because children of this age lack:

    (a) big enough buckets and spades
    (b) suitable damp sand
    (c) perseverance and wrist control
    (d) sufficient encouragement from adults

23. Martin draws a human figure with head, body, arms and legs, in detailed clothing, seated on a horse. He spends ten minutes on it, then screws it up, saying, 'This is rubbish.' He is most likely to be aged:

    (a) between three and four years
    (b) between four and five years
    (c) between five and six years
    (d) between six and seven years

24. Which form of play is most likely to further the acquisition of social skills in the under-fives?

    (a) dolls
    (b) farmyard animals
    (c) sand
    (d) construction sets

25. A wooden tricycle without pedals would be most suitable for a child of:

    (a) six months to one year
    (b) one to two years
    (c) two to three years
    (d) three to four years

26. 'Hairdresser' play is particularly valuable for:

    (a) spreading head infestation
    (b) teaching early science
    (c) teaching adult skills
    (d) encouraging gentle touch and care

27. One of the following is NOT a malleable material. Which is it?

(a) mud
(b) Plasticine
(c) clay
(d) flour

28. Messy play is beneficial to children under five, chiefly because it:

1. offers play with previously forbidden substances
2. gives satisfying end products
3. promotes eye/hand co-ordination
4. encourages a left-to-right eye movement
5. offers a starting point to project work
6. holds a primitive fascination
7. satisfies curiosity about body processes

(a) 1, 6, 7 (b) 1, 3, 5 (c) 2, 4, 5 (d) 4, 6, 7

29. The most important requirement for water play at infant school is that:

(a) it is improvised from household utensils
(b) equipment is bought from an educational supplier
(c) water is coloured and inviting-looking
(d) it offers scope for scientific discovery

30. An adult, sitting with a group of children aged five to seven at a table with twenty coloured counters, is arranging and rearranging the counters. The children are calling out subtotals and totals. They are learning about:

(a) counting, addition, constancy of number
(b) subtraction, division, velocity
(c) multiplication, sets, matching
(d) counting, one-to-one correspondence, addition

31. Shakers, coconut shells, tambourines and drum would all have a part to play in introducing young children to:

(a) pitch
(b) tone
(c) rhythm
(d) melody

32. If a story book has particularly distinctive and enriching language, which of these approaches would you take?

(a) Memorise as much as you can, then tell it.
(b) Tell it in simpler language.
(c) Read it from the book.
(d) Memorise it word-for-word, then tell it.

33. How would you answer a four-year-old doing junk modelling who asks you how many funnels the QE2 has?

    (a) 'Four.'
    (b) 'It's probably two or three.'
    (c) 'I'm not sure but I know where we can look it up.'
    (d) 'Sorry, I don't know.'

34. Which sentence is most likely to encourage a constructive response from a reluctant-to-communicate two-year-old?

    (a) 'What would you like to drink?'
    (b) 'Which would you like – juice or milk?'
    (c) 'Do you want anything to drink?'
    (d) 'Would you like some milk?'

35. Syntax means:

    (a) grammatical structure in sentences
    (b) a type of tack used in woodwork
    (c) a form of income tax
    (d) a behavioural disorder

36. Which procedure would you adopt when introducing a new poem to a group of nursery children?

    (a) Ask the children to repeat it line by line.
    (b) Say it twice all through, then go on to other things.
    (c) Write it out, large, and put it on the wall.
    (d) Keep saying it until they have memorised it perfectly.

37. Which approach should adults encourage small children to adopt towards damaged books?

    (a) Repair them as best they can.
    (b) Bring them to the adult's attention.
    (c) Throw them away.
    (d) Handle them carefully to avoid further damage.

38. A Book Corner in nursery should NEVER be used for:

    (a) a story session for a whole group
    (b) a noisy rhyme session
    (c) a punishment zone for misbehavers
    (d) a poorly child to rest quietly

39. Such traditional tales as *Cinderella, Aladdin, Mother Goose* and many others have a central theme, thought to be worth while imparting to children. It is

    (a) small and defenceless triumphs over big and powerful
    (b) honesty is the best policy
    (c) virtue brings its own reward in the end
    (d) lovers unite and live happily ever after

40. Hans Andersen's story *The Emperor's New Clothes* carries a 'message'. Which is it?

    (a) Never go with strangers.
    (b) Don't follow the crowd unthinkingly.
    (c) Nudity is quite acceptable.
    (d) Patience brings its own reward.

41. A one-and-a-half-year-old boy is always climbing on a window sill. The most effective method of stopping him is to:

    (a) slap his legs whenever he climbs
    (b) remove him every time he climbs
    (c) explain that he will fall and hurt himself
    (d) distract him when he is about to climb

42. A five-year-old child has muscular dystrophy. What is the best response if he asks 'Will I get better?'?

    (a) Change the subject.
    (b) Say 'I don't know.'
    (c) Tell him the truth.
    (d) Say 'Of course you will.'

43. Which one of the following statements is NOT relevant to a list of benefits of family grouping in day nurseries?

    (a) Brothers and sisters can stay together.
    (b) The size of the group makes it dissimilar from unsatisfactory home conditions.
    (c) The nursery officer can get to know each child intimately.
    (d) Children can stay with the same nursery officer for as long as is desirable.

44. An only child will not personally experience:

    (a) sibling rivalry
    (b) mixing with other children
    (c) having to share
    (d) being denied everything he or she wants

45. A child of three years holds his breath until he is blue in the face. What should be done?

    (a) Slap him to make him take a breath.
    (b) Divert his attention to something else.
    (c) Ignore him because he will take a breath.
    (d) Carry out mouth-to-mouth resuscitation.

46. A child who has spiteful tendencies is encouraged to keep a 'kind' book in which is recorded every socially acceptable act. This approach could be said to be:

    (a) punishing him appropriately
    (b) accentuating positive points
    (c) drawing attention to his misdeeds
    (d) letting him experience the consequences of misdeeds

47. A child who experiences little praise or parental pride will probably not develop:

    (a) a good self-image
    (b) good intelligence
    (c) social skills
    (d) defensive attitudes

48. Some nursery children recently witnessed an accident involving a child outside the school. For days afterwards their imaginative play centres on accident scenes, screaming ambulance sirens, stretchers, etc. The staff in charge would be advised to:

    (a) let them work it out of their systems in this way
    (b) explain that it's all over now, and that they are not to worry
    (c) divert their play to happier themes
    (d) say they are tired of this game and want to see a change

49. When parents of a nursery child are undergoing a break-up of their relationship it is helpful if they:

    (a) use one member of staff as a counsellor/confidante
    (b) keep the child at home for a while
    (c) outline the situation to the person in charge of the child's group
    (d) get the child to explain the situation to staff

50. Linda, four years old, keeps talking about her recently-dead Granny. The staff at school would be advised to:

    (a) divert the conversation to happier topics
    (b) listen sympathetically
    (c) reassure her that Grandad won't die as well
    (d) explain that Granny is in heaven looking down at her

51. A six-year-old child begins pulling out quantities of her own hair, and also smearing her faeces round the toilet. This could be described as:

    (a) exploratory play
    (b) play with malleable substances
    (c) regressive behaviour
    (d) bizarre behaviour

52. Sudden infant death syndrome is to be found in all socio-economic classes. This statement is:

    (a) true
    (b) untrue
    (c) used to be true but is no longer
    (d) misleading

53. You might use a playpen for an older child (of approximately three to six):

    (a) when she is in a temper and needs to be isolated
    (b) to make her feel like a baby as a punishment for behaving like one
    (c) to keep her away from the baby if she is in a boisterous mood
    (d) to enable her to play with a precious toy that baby might damage

54. A two-and-a-half-year-old child in hospital who shows signs of upset at separation from parents is probably:

    (a) mature enough mentally to realise he will soon be with them again
    (b) grieving inside
    (c) happily diverted by new play experiences
    (d) consciously putting a brave face on things

55. A five-year-old whose single-parent mother has recently remarried is likely to be experiencing:

    (a) some feelings of jealousy and resentment
    (b) total pleasure that now she's got a father
    (c) much more in the way of material possessions
    (d) disgust at her mother's sexuality

56. Extended families are comparatively rare nowadays in our society. The chief reason is:

    (a) that houses are smaller
    (b) that grandparents live longer
    (c) socio-economic mobility
    (d) understanding of psychology

14

57. You would normally expect a child from a Hindu family not to eat:

    (a) eggs
    (b) meat
    (c) fish
    (d) vegetables

58. The children of travellers may possibly experience:

    (a) lack of contact with other children
    (b) lack of extended family contacts
    (c) lack of education
    (d) lack of consistent health care

59. You would normally expect a child from a Moslem family not to eat:

    (a) pork
    (b) beef
    (c) lamb
    (d) chicken

60. Child abuse is most likely to stem from

    (a) unemployment of parent(s)
    (b) emotional problems of parent(s)
    (c) one-parent families
    (d) financial problems of parent(s)

61. What are the three most important reasons for home/school involvement?

    1. fund-raising
    2. socialisation
    3. parent power
    4. relief of teachers
    5. improved school performance of child
    6. consistency of handling
    7. mutual respect by all carers
    8. spread of information

    (a) 1, 3, 5   (b) 5, 6, 7   (c) 2, 6, 8   (d) 3, 5, 7

62. Kosher food is:

    (a) food that has been slaughtered/prepared according to Talmudic ritual
    (b) food that has not been slaughtered/prepared according to Talmudic ritual
    (c) vegetarian food
    (d) high-fibre 'health' foods

63. About a quarter of today's young children will have experienced living in a single-parent family before they reach age sixteen. This statement is:

    (a) true
    (b) untrue
    (c) used to be true but is no longer
    (d) may be true some time in the future

64. The principle of the National Health Service is that:

    (a) everything is free
    (b) everybody pays what they can afford
    (c) medical care is available to all
    (d) minimum standards of care are maintained

65. A professional visitor to an infant school is overheard commenting that a four-year-old is 'disfluent'. The person is probably a:

    (a) speech therapist
    (b) audiometrician
    (c) dentist
    (d) social worker

66. The NSPCC Young League consists of:

    (a) young parents being supported by NSPCC
    (b) children who raise funds for NSPCC
    (c) children who have formed the casework of NSPCC officers
    (d) children of NSPCC officers

67. 'The induction of abortion is legal under certain conditions.' This statement is:

    (a) true throughout the world
    (b) untrue throughout Europe
    (c) true throughout the United Kingdom
    (d) untrue throughout the world

68. Who is responsible for providing accommodation for homeless families with children?

    (a) Social Services
    (b) Local Authority Housing Department
    (c) Environmental Health Department
    (d) Social Security

16

69. A health visitor must be:

    (a) a trained social worker
    (b) a trained nurse
    (c) a married woman
    (d) a single woman

70. In the United Kingdom, advice on contraception is freely available to:

    (a) married couples only
    (b) women with medical problems only
    (c) everyone
    (d) everyone over sixteen

71. 'Irretrievable breakdown' is a phrase used when:

    (a) a couple is seeking divorce
    (b) a couple is seeking a separation
    (c) one parent is seeking access to a child
    (d) a single parent is claiming maintenance

72. 'Statementing' is carried out only for:

    (a) children with a mental handicap
    (b) children who have hearing problems
    (c) children who have special needs
    (d) children who have health problems

73. If a nursery nurse student is given permission to take some nursery school children to the local library, the legal responsibility for their safe conduct rests with:

    (a) herself
    (b) the children's parents
    (c) her course tutor
    (d) the head teacher of the nursery school

74. A nursery nurse working at an infant school hears rumours that her role is going to be altogether changed. She should:

    (a) ask her closest friend on the staff if it is true
    (b) make an appointment with the head to discuss her future career
    (c) tell the head that the school is abuzz with rumours about her
    (d) wait and see and put up with it if necessary

75. The most important aspect of the nursery officer's role as supervisor to NNEB students is:

   (a) criticism and praise
   (b) inspecting their observation work
   (c) being a role model of good child care practice herself
   (d) giving them full information about each child's background

76. A mother of a four-and-a-half-year-old girl in a reception class complains that all the child does in school is play. The teacher/nursery nurse should:

   (a) provide the mother with relevant reading material
   (b) try to explain the day to her
   (c) tell her she is quite wrong
   (d) invite her to stay and participate in activities

77. A curriculum vitae is:

   (a) information about a person's education, experience, career and hobbies
   (b) the curriculum of an infant school
   (c) the motto of a teachers' union
   (d) the Latin name of a poisonous plant

78. How would you deal with a mother who expects her child to bring home a painting or piece of craft work, from nursery school, every day, as he used to do at playgroup?

   (a) Tell her you do things differently at nursery school.
   (b) Urge her child to produce what she expects, to keep her happy.
   (c) Invite her in to see other activities that do not result in end products.
   (d) Arrange things so that the whole class produces something to take home at least twice a week.

79. On her first day at work, a nursery nurse is approached by a union representative and asked to join. She should

   (a) agree, in order to be accepted quickly
   (b) say that she is investigating several relevant unions and will make a decision soon
   (c) agree for fear of causing trouble
   (d) refuse because membership of any union is her own affair

80. The employer of a nanny criticises her for letting dirty dishes pile up in the kitchen to await her return from work. The nanny would be advised to:

(a) explain politely that play is much more important than domestic chores
(b) acknowledge that this must be a depressing sight and agree to do it as she goes along
(c) explain politely that she is there to be with the child at all times, not doing domestic duties
(d) hand in her notice

EXAMPLE 1 OF AN ESSAY PAPER

You will have three hours for the whole paper, and must answer one question from each of Sections A, B, C and D. The maximum marks for these are shown in the right hand column.

SECTION A

Marks

A1 Why do babies cry?   5
Describe in detail how you would deal with one of the causes of crying in the case of a seven-month-old baby.   5

or

A2 Road accidents are a common cause of death or injury in children under seven years.
Why is this?   4
How can the nursery nurse play a part in road safety education?   6

SECTION B

B1 Using examples, describe how play with dolls and soft toys can contribute to the all-round development of children in the years between infancy and age seven.   10

or

B2 A three-year-old is admitted to nursery school, apparently unable to communicate.
What might be the reasons for this?   5
How could you help him or her?   5

SECTION C

C1 The average British family consists of 1.7 children.
How may growing up as an only child affect his or her development?   6
What factors outside the home are important to such a child?   4

or

C2 Richard, two years old, has protruding ears. His mother is anxious for these to be corrected as soon as possible, which will involve an operation in hospital.
When would be the best age to do this?   2
How would you as his nanny prepare him for hospitalisation?   8

SECTION D

D1 Besides practical training, and vocational studies, there are many other aspects to the NNEB course.
Which do you think will prove to be most useful to you in the future?   10

or

D2 You are employed as a nanny to a single-parent family consisting of working mother and children – a boy of two years and a girl of four years. Father has access once a week.
How could you help all the members of this family cope with the situation?   10

Here is one way in which a good candidate might answer Sections A, B, C and D.

SECTION A

A1: Plan

		Indications
WHY DO BABIES CRY?	Communication	speech
	Survival	
	Needs not satisfied	*see below*
PHYSICAL NEEDS	Food and drink	hungry, thirsty
	Cleanliness	needs nappy change
	Rest	tired
	Exercise	frustrated
	Warmth	too cold or too hot
	Good health	ill
	Protection	in pain

21

MENTAL NEEDS	Security	feels insecure
	Affection	wants a cuddle
	Stimulation ⎫	bored
	Social contacts ⎭	
	Independence	frustrated
SEVEN-MONTH-OLD CRYING	Find cause	*Action*
	Most likely	comfort
	teething	teething ring
		cream for sore skin
		extra fluids
		teething jelly
		GP for ears

Essay

Crying is very important to a baby's survival because in his early days it is his only means of communication. At the moment of birth most babies will cry lustily when they take their first breath. By this means a baby inflates and clears his lungs.

Early in life a baby learns that crying will nearly always elicit some response because it is a distress signal and very few adults will resist the urge to do something about it. Later the baby develops different types of crying and this is the true beginning of speech. It is possible quite soon for his mother or nurse to differentiate between types of crying and to respond appropriately. For instance, there is the very urgent cry when his feed is due, and the gradually diminishing whimper as he goes off to sleep. Later, when he can convey his needs in other ways, a baby will still resort to crying if he is in distress or his need is very urgent.

Crying usually indicates that one of the baby's essential needs requires attention. His mother or nurse can generally identify the problem by a process of observation, detection and elimination. For instance, if it is a very hot day and the baby was fed about an hour ago, he could simply be thirsty and need a drink. Or he could just be too hot and need some clothing removed.

There are numerous reasons why a baby cries and it is possible to list the main probabilities in descending order of importance and to link them to the needs of the baby.

Food: The baby could be hungry or thirsty.
Security: This can be physical or mental. Fear of falling when held insecurely will often cause a baby to cry. If there are problems of stress in a baby's home, he may sense the tension and respond by crying.

Affection: A baby can feel lonely and long for a demonstration of affection.

Good health: The baby may be ill or in pain. Most commonly this can be caused by colic in a baby under three months of age and by teething in a baby over three months.

Rest: Many small babies will cry for a short while when they are put down to sleep, so it is always worth waiting five minutes to see if the baby will settle and sleep.

Warmth: If a baby is too hot or too cold he will cry.

Exercise: Sometimes when a baby is lying tucked into his pram in one position he will cry because he cannot move freely. This baby would enjoy being placed on the floor in order to exercise.

Stimulation and social contacts: Many babies become bored and frustrated through lack of stimulation. Because their concentration span is limited they will need changing stimuli.

Cleanliness: In his early days a baby will cry because he has a wet or soiled nappy. Later he will learn to tolerate that situation.

If I were looking after a seven-month-old baby who was crying, I would try to find the cause quickly by mentally going through all the possibilities and by using my knowledge of the baby to narrow down the choices. By the time the baby was seven months old a mother or nurse would know whether this was one who was easily frustrated and cried at any setback or was a placid baby who was happy most of the time. As this baby is said to be usually contented, I would assume at first that she was in pain from teething, especially if her appearance backed up the assumption.

Teething babies are often very miserable. They push their fists into their mouths and rub their gums and often pull their ears. They usually dribble all the time and often have sore chins from the constant wetness. Sometimes there is a patch of red on one or both cheeks. When they suck on the breast or bottle they may suddenly scream in pain as they purse their lips so that, although eager for the feed, they may stop sucking for a while. When cuddled and comforted they will quieten but soon resume their crying. They may try to bite on anything to hand – the mother's or the nurse's finger or jaw, the rails of the cot or any toys. When food is given on a spoon they will bite hard on it and may cry as they eat the food because of the pain.

To help the baby I would give frequent drinks of boiled water to replace the fluid lost in salivation. I would also apply cream, such as zinc and castor oil, to her chin to relieve the soreness. A hard rusk and a teething ring can be given for the baby to bite upon. Teething jelly rubbed gently into the gums may bring some relief. Above all, I would spend a lot of time comforting her and I would also try to distract her from the pain by playing with her.

If she was not any better after twenty-four hours had elapsed, I would take her to her doctor and ask him to check on her ears and throat to ensure that there was no other reason for her misery. The doctor might prescribe a pain reliever if he felt it was necessary.

A2: Plan

WHY ACCIDENTS HAPPEN	ROAD SAFETY EDUCATION

1. Nature of child:
    irresponsible
    unpredictable
    poor concentration
    too small to see traffic
	Teach child to think first.
	Talk about traffic – cars, lorries, motorbikes, etc.
	Get people in to talk:
	    'Lollipop lady'
	    Road Safety Officer

2. Child's lack of experience:
    inability to judge speeds
    ignorance of dangers
    inability to understand verbal warnings
	Give experience:
	    cars and model layout
	    junk modelling
	    board games
	    practice

3. Child copies adults' incorrect behaviour	Always show by example, e.g. cross roads correctly.
4. Given responsibility when too young	Always accompany children under seven years. Take children out on visits and teach them how to cross roads safely. Remember security – doors, gates, ball playing, etc.

N.B. When answering the second part of the question, it would be best to use one setting, e.g. nursery/infant school/nanny and discuss how you would educate this particular group instead of generalising over the entire age range. Use your own experience where possible, for instance beginning '. . . when I was working with a group of five to seven-year-old children in an infant school, I . . .'

SECTION B

B1: Plan

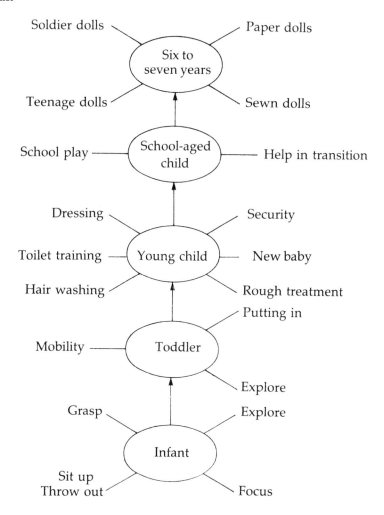

Essay

From the age of only about six or seven weeks, my nephew showed a lot of interest in the soft toy bunny which was hung up in his cot. He used to frown in concentration as he focused on it. Later, he would make a swipe at it with one hand, and be fascinated to see it move. It probably encouraged him, a little later on, to sit up so that he could

25

grasp it. He would explore the furry taste and feel with his mouth. At about eight months, he would delight in throwing it out of his pram, and enjoy the attention this brought him when a passer-by would return it to him with a kind word.

I have noticed that toddlers often involve dolls in their games of 'putting in' and 'taking out', or taking things for rides. My niece at eighteen months used to put her little soft toy doll inside a saucepan she was allowed to play with on the kitchen floor. She would then cover it up with a saucepan lid and, grinning, would play a sort of 'Now you see it, now you don't' game with any adult who was nearby. She had clearly grasped the idea of object permanence by this stage.

By about two she used to put several dolls in her baby-walker and take them round the garden. 'Babies go walk,' she used to explain happily, as she trundled round, all the time becoming more agile and confident with this stable aid to her walking.

At about three, she developed a great fondness for one particular baby doll – her 'Funny'. She was not bothered about dressing or undressing it, and at times would treat it roughly, dragging it around by an arm or its hair, and sometimes venting her temper on it, especially if she was in trouble over something. But she always wanted it beside her at bedtime, and it was a great source of comfort whenever she had to go to the doctor's, or stay at a different house.

It was at about this time that her mother had another baby, and Jessica was obviously experiencing all the usual mixed and powerful emotions. Her parents had taken the wise precaution of buying her a new and life-like baby doll to care for at the same times that the mother was intimately involved in feeding, bathing, etc. This certainly helped to minimise her 'left out' feeling, and prevented her seeking attention and being trying at these times, as she imitated her mother's actions, thus also learning the mother role. The baby doll wet its nappy, which fascinated Jessica, and probably helped her to avoid regression of this kind. Her new-found gentleness was now extended to other dolls as well; even poor old 'Funny' came in for some TLC! Dressing baby doll properly also gave her useful practice in fasteners, 'inside out', etc., which was applicable to her own clothes. She still used to make a great fuss at hair-washing time. Her mother discovered that insisting that baby Jane had her hair washed first meant that Jessica's interest was captured, and she would forget to protest about her own.

When I was training at an infant school, several of the new children, boys as well as girls, would at first bring in their favourite doll or soft toy – teddies being the most common. This use of a transitional object helped the children to make the commitment to school more easily. The teacher would treat the dolls with respect, and put them on a high shelf where their owners could see them, and where no-one could damage them. As the children settled and became confident, so their need for their dolls faded.

One mother told me that Sarah would set up a real 'school' play situation when she returned home in the evening, with all her dolls, teddies and soft toys. From this – discreetly – observed play, Sarah's mother learned more about what Sarah had been doing that day than by direct questions, to which she did not respond well. It even came about that Sarah's mother realised, through this play, that Sarah was very agitated about school dinners, and, once having realised this, she was able to seek help.

Children at the top end of the infant school loved their teenage dolls. They engaged in wonderful imaginative play, the language they used to describe the various dolls' outfits and accessories being surprisingly sophisticated and elaborate. They would be quite competitive in their acquisition of new accessories. I think this was a way of coping with their envy of older teenage siblings, or hero-worship of pop stars seen on television. Soldier dolls were also popular, appearing to satisfy the boys' love of action and adventure.

Some of the children used to make cardboard dolls and paper clothes – quite an exacting task – and also sometimes sewn dolls, which required a good deal of manual dexterity and concentration. The finished products were often extremely ugly to adult eyes, but the children took enormous pride in them, and would play dotingly with them afterwards.

B2: Plan

CAUSES		
	Deafness	Over-protected by parents
	Catarrh	Twins
	Lack of stimulation	'Spoken for' by siblings
	Shyness	Low intelligence
	Overwhelmed by nursery school	Autism
	Non-English speaking	Malformation of one of the speech mechanisms
	Immaturity	Brain damage
	Trauma	

HELP		
	Discuss with mother and include her in strategies	One special friend
		One special adult
	Hearing test and other specialised help	Language activities, e.g. finger plays, with group
	One-to-one attention and careful listening	Other forms of stimulation/ communication, e.g. music, movement
	Close observation	
	Good model yourself	Help with hearing aid if applicable
	Make him ask for things, etc.	

Suitable play material, e.g.   Patience, sensitivity
Home Corner, puppets   Praise, encouragement
Encourage mixing

SECTION C

C1: Plan

DISADVANTAGES	Resentment	Ignorance of babies
	Life without siblings	Over-protected
	No ally	Anxiety
	Possessive about toys	Risk at break-up
	Loneliness	Too close
	Envy	Resentment of new
	Too much trouble	partner
ADVANTAGES	Satisfaction	Friendship skills
	Material benefits/	Language development
	opportunities	One-to-one
	New clothes	
FACTORS	M and T Club,	Nursery school
	Playgroup, Sunday	Preparation for infant
	School	school
	Informal arrangements	Extended family
	Clinics	

Essay

The only child suffers a number of disadvantages. He may not appreciate the reasons underlying his parents' decision that their family should stop at one; he may regard them as selfish, and as deliberately denying his need for companionship and playmates, whom he may perceive as wholly desirable.

He will probably miss out on the need to share, the cut and thrust, give and take of life with siblings. He will escape the teasing, the rivalry, the private jokes, shared experiences of family life that often make for much affection, feelings of solidarity, security and joy, in childhood and later. When he feels he has been unfairly dealt with by parents, he will have no-one to turn to for support or comfort. His toys and belongings will be entirely his own, and he may become obsessively preoccupied with them.

He may feel lonely in school holidays, at weekends and when on holiday with his parents. He may look with envy on 'gangs' of children and young people, and become withdrawn. If he is not naturally outgoing, he may dread, or tire of, the effort constantly needed to make and keep friends, so he may become a loner.

He will not undergo the – often traumatic – experience of accepting a younger sibling into his family. Therefore he will miss out on all baby routines, the need for gentleness to small defenceless beings, and the character-building process of adjusting to others. He may be over-protected by his parents, or become anxious or resentful because he is the sole focus of their hopes, fears and expectations.

If his parents break up or become ill, this will be more traumatic for the only child than for siblings, who have one another to cling to.

If he is already in a single-parent family, the child and his parent may become unnaturally close. The child may have to grow up too quickly, and be the confidant and constant companion of the remaining parent, particularly if he or she is of the opposite sex. If that parent enters a new relationship, the introduction of someone else could be threatening and resented.

On the other hand, the only child will enjoy certain advantages. If both parents are present, the small family today is usually the result of a conscious decision by the parents, and this should generate an atmosphere of satisfaction within which the child will grow up. Probably financial and economic considerations determined the parents' decision, so the child – although it does not follow that he will be over-indulged – will be unlikely to go short of material advantages. Sufficient money, besides bringing basic essentials, such as adequate housing, food and clothing, also buys social advantages and opportunities – for example, access to clubs, social circles and dancing lessons, and being able to go on horizon-widening holidays, go to camps, take part in foreign exchanges, etc. If the family runs a car, outings – both the 'fun' kind and the more 'educational' kind – can be frequent, providing enjoyment, and alerting the child to many interests.

Not for this child the disappointment and possible humiliation of 'hand-me-down' clothes, nor the risk of precious toys, books and other belongings being 'borrowed' or damaged by siblings. Privacy should not be a problem either.

Because he has no ready-made companions, the only child will have to 'work at' friendships, and may develop skills, such as listening, that will be an asset all his life. He may be especially close to his parents, and the fact of being largely with adults will probably enhance his language abilities. He will enjoy much one-to-one attention.

Unfortunately, many of the advantages listed above may not be available if this only child is growing up in one of the millions of single-parent families today. It is possible that poverty, stress, social isolation and low parental self-esteem may overshadow the whole of the child's life.

The parent or parents of an only child should take steps from an early stage to ensure that he has plenty of contact with other children and interests outside the home. At Mother and Toddler Clubs, Playgroup, Sunday School – or equivalent – the child will experience initiating relationships, sharing toys, waiting turns, changing roles, enduring delays, needing to be protective and gentle to smaller children, developing a healthy respect for older, bigger children. His parent or parents will also develop more realistic expectations of him by seeing his peers in action.

In addition the parents can arrange informal reciprocal play periods for their children at each other's houses. This can be beneficial because sharing his own belongings on his own territory may at first come particularly hard to an only child. Visits can also be made to places like Health Clinics and Health Centres, which will provide an additional interest for such a child.

A nursery school class place would naturally be of great advantage to this child. If he is unlucky in this respect, the big step of starting infant school will need careful preparation, through preliminary visits, situation books and casual references to all the interesting things he will be doing.

Another source of contact for only children is the extended family, particularly cousins, who can offer a great deal to them and give them a feeling of belonging to a distinctive unit.

C2: Plan

BEST AGE
Three to four years.   Why?
  Able to leave mother
  Can relate to other people
  Can understand verbal explanation
  Not yet at school – not interrupting education
              – not being teased about ears

PREPARATIONS
Explain simply – and repeat
  Reassure
  Arrange to go into hospital with him
  Visit hospital ward – sometimes preparation
  classes to attend
  Situation books
  Play people – doctors and nurses
  Doctor's outfit
  Involve in packing suitcase
  Take favourite toy

30

SECTION D

D1: Plan

NEW SKILLS	NATURE	WRITTEN AND SPOKEN ENGLISH
Art	Conservation	Self-confidence
Craft	Knowledge	Interview technique
Music	Dangers	Letter-writing
Self-confidence		Reading for pleasure
Resourcefulness		
Projecting		
Techniques		

STUDENT RESPONSIBILITIES	GROWING-UP PERIOD
Organising	Individual help
Diplomacy	Example to follow
Relationships	Fun
Good example	Friendships
	Enthusiasm for study

Essay

I seem to have learned many new skills at college, which I know will be relevant and useful to my work with children. I have learned several different art techniques with paint, printing, dyeing, etc. Some of these can be directly introduced to children, while others have given me personally more self-confidence. I never used to be any good at school art, and I approached the subject at college with feelings of failure, which I have been helped to overcome. I know now that proper tuition in techniques, together with perseverance, can result in a fair degree of achievement, and I hope I shall remember this when I meet older children who are critical of their own efforts, or who fear to try new approaches. I have also learned how best to enhance children's work by mounting, display, lettering and so on.

In craft, too, I have enjoyed trying out many new techniques such as woodwork, canework, pottery and weaving. I may even be able to make some play and other equipment for the children I work with. However, I intend to keep my cradle and quilt strictly for my own family! Also in craft activities I have been encouraged to be resourceful in improvising, and using natural materials such as bark, feathers and 'junk'. This will undoubtedly be useful if I am looking for 'rainy day' activities as a nanny, or maybe when helping to run a playgroup on limited funds, and, of course, when I have children of my own.

During the study of man in his environment, I have become really interested in wild life and conservation. I never thought much about this before, but now I am determined to pass on my concern about threatened species to children, and educate them in playing their part. I have also learned many useful facts about poisonous plants and berries, and feel more able to spot potential dangers to children. I have a much greater store of knowledge about trees, animals, insects, so that I am better prepared to answer children's endless questions.

I have benefited – I hope! – from extra practice at written English. I now feel more confident about writing a good letter of application for a job, or writing a review on a child, or a report on a student in my charge. I have in addition been introduced to new reading matter – away from examination pressure – and now really enjoy reading for pleasure.

Spoken English, and passing a national examination in this, seemed a nerve-racking prospect at first, but I am glad that I did it. I can now speak up in a large-ish group, and put a point of view coherently and firmly, without being aggressive. We have also done role play for interviews, which has been illuminating.

Musical activities, while failing to achieve the impossible in giving me a beautiful voice, or real instrumental skill, have helped me to project. I now appreciate that even *my* voice, maybe accompanied by a few guitar chords, can convey sufficient enthusiasm to bring enjoyment to children.

Student Union activities have provided another aspect of the course. Being a group 'rep' enabled me to get to know other students and tutors well and quickly, and to see the point of a lot that went on. I had to be quite diplomatic, yet loyal to my group. I also felt I had to give a lead in organising my time and work commitments so that I submitted assignments on time, and did not let my SU responsibilities, or my social life or Saturday job, become excuses for not putting college work first.

When we tried to organise a dance, I learned a lot about planning, costing, and the difficulties of pleasing everyone, and drumming up support.

I got involved in some careers talks to secondary schools, and it seemed strange but gratifying to return to my own former school in a different role. I also helped at some admission interviews, which again boosted my self-confidence, and helped me for job interviews.

I think that just being a student has been a marvellous experience. It seemed to bridge the gap between schoolgirl and adult. I have benefited from a lot of one-to-one teaching and counselling time by tutors, and I hope that when I am training students myself I shall remember this.

Last of all, college days have been such fun that they will always be a happy memory for me. I shall certainly encourage young friends or my own children to enter further education. I hope to continue study in some form or another all my life. And I also hope to retain the wonderful friends I have made.

D2: Plan

HELP TO CHILDREN	Simple explanation of situation.
	Situation books.
	Reassurance – they are not to blame, both parents love them.
	Establishment of secure routine and home life around mother's job.
	Make allowance for behaviour irregularities around access occasions.
HELP TO MOTHER	Acceptance of situation.
	Discussions with her about children's routine.
	Cooperation about access arrangements.
	Emotional support.
	Tact.
HELP TO FATHER	Acceptance of situation.
	Be pleasant.
	Maintain respect for him in children's eyes.
	Suggest places for him to visit, or cooperate over arrangements with home.
	Prepare children, physically and emotionally, for visits.
	Show interest afterwards.
HELP TO BOTH PARENTS	Avoid 'taking sides' or making judgements.

EXAMPLE 2 OF A MULTIPLE CHOICE PAPER

1. When you touch a two-week-old baby's cheek, he turns and sucks your finger. This is because:

    (a) he is very hungry
    (b) he wants to bite you
    (c) it is a reflex action
    (d) he is very thirsty

2. What is the earliest age for a baby to participate in 'Pat-a-cake'?

    (a) four months
    (b) six months
    (c) ten months
    (d) sixteen months

3. By what age is a premature baby expected to catch up with normal development?

    (a) one year
    (b) one and a half years
    (c) two years
    (d) three years

4. A child of two years should be able to:

    (a) put two to three words together
    (b) use six words with meaning
    (c) tell you his or her address
    (d) tell you the primary colours

5. The main advantage of disposable nappies is:

    (a) cheapness
    (b) prevention of nappy rash
    (c) ease of changing
    (d) reduction of workload

6. Which food is the best source of iron?

    (a) green vegetables
    (b) milk
    (c) bread
    (d) eggs

7. What would you consider to be the most effective method of teaching children of three and four years about road safety?

    (a) Make a board game for them to play.
    (b) Improvise a road layout outside, and guide children's movements on wheeled vehicles.
    (c) Give them a floor road layout and small vehicles.
    (d) Tell them a story in which a three-year-old meets with a serious accident.

8. Mobiles for babies should be characterised by:

    1. use of improvised household articles
    2. bright colours
    3. interesting shapes
    4. capable of movement in breeze
    5. textural qualities
    6. being placed near enough for child to touch

    (a) 2, 3, 4   (b) 1, 5, 6   (c) 2, 4, 6   (d) 1, 4, 5

9. A child is said to be growing along the 'third centile'. This means that:

    (a) her growth is the same as that of the top 3 per cent of children
    (b) her growth is abnormally slow
    (c) she is growing too fat
    (d) she is small but growing normally

10. What is plaque?

    (a) an infectious disease of the stomach
    (b) a skin disease
    (c) bacteria and food debris in the mouth
    (d) medicine in tablet form

11. Many parents are reluctant to have their children immunised against whooping cough. This is because:

    (a) many children get a sore arm
    (b) the injection hurts the child
    (c) they do not think it is necessary
    (d) they are afraid of vaccine damage

12. If you were told a child in 'your' nursery class came from a family of vegans, it would mean:

    (a) they are of a nationality other than British
    (b) they eat everything but meat
    (c) they do not eat meat, fish, eggs, cheese, milk or any animal products
    (d) they belong to a little-known religious sect

13. Deficiency diseases are caused by:

    (a) poor hygiene
    (b) poor diet
    (c) poor sleep
    (d) poor general care

14. A genetic disease is said to be 'sex-linked'. This means a disease which:

    (a) only affects girls
    (b) is passed on during sexual intercourse
    (c) is passed on from mother to son
    (d) develops when a child reaches sexual maturity

15. A child has a heart defect which will require surgery. How should you treat him?

    (a) Make him rest as much as possible.
    (b) Let him rest when he wants to.
    (c) Make allowances for bad behaviour.
    (d) Let him have all his own way.

16. In which way can AIDS be passed from person to person?

    (a) shaking hands
    (b) sexual contact
    (c) using the same towel
    (d) breathing the same air

17. What is the immediate first-aid treatment for a scald?

    (a) Cool the area with cold water.
    (b) Apply anti-burn cream.
    (c) Cover with a dry, sterile dressing.
    (d) Take the child to hospital.

18. What is the best time to transfer a child from a cot to a bed?

    (a) when the new baby arrives
    (b) when he is ready to do so
    (c) when he is eighteen months old
    (d) as soon as possible after his first birthday

36

19. A health visitor visits to:

    (a) give advice about health care
    (b) ensure that a child is not battered
    (c) check that the home is clean
    (d) make mothers attend the clinic

20. Babies are sometimes fed on soya milk. This is usually because:

    (a) they do not like other milks
    (b) they are allergic to cow's milk
    (c) their parents are vegans
    (d) they have phenylketonuria

21. You want to buy a teddy bear for a child's second birthday.
    Which are the most important considerations?

    1. size
    2. cuddliness
    3. clothes that the child can take off and on
    4. safely-secured eyes
    5. workmanship for durability
    6. variety of fastenings
    7. it is one of a set that can be added to later

    (a) 2, 4, 6, 7   (b) 1, 2, 4, 5   (c) 3, 5, 6, 7   (d) 1, 2, 3, 4

22. 'Put it in the middle.' 'How many pieces would you like?' 'We
    need a large packet of soap powder.' 'These shoes are getting
    too small for you.'
    These are all examples of adult language that the child has heard
    from earliest days; they provide a useful working background
    of:

    (a) mathematical understanding
    (b) social skills
    (c) emotional security
    (d) personal relationships

23. She likes picture books and simple stories, and enjoys the
    rhythm of nursery rhymes. Her favourite toys are a dustpan and
    brush, a hammer toy, a shopping basket and a small rag doll.
    She is likely to be:

    (a) two to three years old
    (b) three to four years old
    (c) four to five years old
    (d) five to six years old

24. Two four-year-old children are moving 'play people' and rubber dinosaurs around a tank of sand and water. They are using these materials chiefly:

(a) to discover early scientific principles
(b) to play imaginatively
(c) to make a legitimate mess
(d) to understand capacity

25. Water for playing with should be coloured:

(a) always, to make it more interesting
(b) yellow, to help children with toilet training problems
(c) white, to stimulate imaginative play
(d) sometimes, to vary play possibilities

26. Home Corner play offers learning opportunities in several of the following areas:

1. mathematics
2. language
3. cookery
4. density
5. nature study
6. direction
7. social interaction
8. role reversal

(a) 1, 3, 4, 6   (b) 2, 4, 5, 7   (c) 1, 5, 6, 7   (d) 1, 2, 7, 8

27. Making bark rubbings will give small children a good idea of:

(a) symmetry
(b) the seasonal cycle
(c) pattern in nature
(d) need for accuracy

28. The story of *The Three Bears* can help small children to become more aware of:

(a) the dangers of eating food that is too hot
(b) the danger of boasting
(c) comparative size
(d) the life cycle of bears

29. Which question would be most likely to lead to a worthwhile discussion with a group of three-to-four-year-olds to whom you have just told the story of *The Three Bears*?

(a) What would you do if you found someone asleep in your bed?
(b) How many people have porridge for breakfast?
(c) What was the name of the little girl in the story?
(d) How many bears were there in the story?

30. Which question is most likely to calm and re-invigorate sand play that has become noisy and over-boisterous?

    (a) Why are you making so much noise?
    (b) Who can make the best sand-castle?
    (c) How did you make such a huge castle?
    (d) Who will help me clear up?

31. How would you answer a four-year-old who asks why leaves fall off trees in autumn?

    (a) 'Because it makes a pretty carpet for the ground.'
    (b) 'Because it provides a winter home for insects.'
    (c) 'It is to do with the seasonal cycle of growth.'
    (d) 'In the winter, there is not enough food for leaves.'

32. *Sleeping Beauty*, besides being a good story, can offer children additional interesting food for thought on which of these topics?

    (a) the dangers of spinning
    (b) the passing of time
    (c) the need for patience
    (d) fate catches up with evil people

33. Young children's books in the home should be stored:

    (a) in a toy box or cupboard, along with other possessions
    (b) on separate shelves at child height
    (c) on separate shelves out of reach
    (d) in a strong duffle bag

34. Visual aids should be used as part of story-telling to young children:

    (a) always, as they give a visual focus
    (b) never, because children should be encouraged to use their imagination
    (c) sometimes, if the story lends itself to this approach
    (d) only if the story-teller is so nervous that she needs something to hold

35. Books for children as young as one year should be:

    (a) made of fabric that is washable
    (b) made of card or strengthened paper
    (c) made of card 'concertina'
    (d) made of ordinary paper

36. Puppets are particularly therapeutic for which children?

    (a) children with learning difficulties
    (b) shy children
    (c) highly imaginative children
    (d) aggressive children

37. Which action is it advisable to take when preparing children's paintings for display?

    (a) Double or triple mount every one, on backing paper.
    (b) Trim off parts which do not fit in with the current group 'theme'.
    (c) Leave them entirely as they are and put them direct on to walls.
    (d) Back or frame them simply, without detracting from the children's pictures.

38. Listening to extracts of classical music might be introduced to four-year-olds in order to:

    (a) inspire creative writing
    (b) replace outdoor play on a rainy day
    (c) convey a mood under discussion
    (d) provide accompaniment to their percussion instrument playing

39. 'Me do it! Timmy pay ball.' These sentences are most likely to be spoken by a child of:

    (a) two years
    (b) three years
    (c) four years
    (d) five years

40. 'What is it?' is usually an inappropriate question to ask a child about his painting because:

    (a) he may take too long to tell you
    (b) the subject of his painting is probably too personal to speak about
    (c) he only wants praise, not conversation
    (d) he will infer that only adult-recognisable pictures are acceptable

41. A four-year-old child is scared of a dark cupboard. How can you help her overcome this?

   (a) Make her go into the cupboard alone.
   (b) Fix a light in the cupboard.
   (c) Explain that only babies are scared.
   (d) Go into the cupboard with her.

42. Temper tantrums in a two-year-old mean that:

   (a) he is frustrated
   (b) he is naughty
   (c) he is bad-tempered
   (d) he is not well

43. A three-year-old child refuses to eat her dinner. What is the best way to deal with this?

   (a) Make her sit at the table until she eats it.
   (b) Give her a set time to eat and then give up.
   (c) Play a game with her to get her to eat.
   (d) Change the meal to something she likes.

44. A three-year-old child is soon to start nursery. Which of the following steps would be most beneficial?

   (a) Tell him he is a big boy now and going to nursery.
   (b) Ask an older child to come in and talk about it.
   (c) Pick your time and give him a long talking to.
   (d) Show him story/picture books about school.

45. A five-year-old still wets his bed at night. This means that:

   (a) he is very naughty
   (b) he is dirty
   (c) he is immature
   (d) he is abnormal

46. Which of the following statements would NOT be appropriate to prepare a three-year-old for a new sibling?

   (a) 'You'll be able to help Mummy with the baby.'
   (b) 'You'll be able to show your baby off to your friends.'
   (c) 'Isn't Mummy lucky to have you to help her with baby?'
   (d) 'You'll have a little playmate.'

47. A four-year-old is tearful about going back into school after her first weekend since starting. It would be helpful for the parent/nanny to:

(a) explain kindly that she's got to go to school for another twelve years yet
(b) explain sympathetically that she hated school too when she was a child
(c) give her extra crisps and sweets to take with her
(d) arrange that she takes with her an item of interest found or received at the weekend

48. A six-year-old brings to school a poor quality book given to him by his granny and consisting mainly of strip cartoons and violent happenings; he asks you to 'read it to the whole class.' It would be best to:

(a) suggest that Granny comes to the school to find out about more suitable books
(b) say 'I'm sorry, I'm afraid there won't be time today.'
(c) show the class the pictures, but make up different text as you go
(d) suggest that the child reads it to a group of chosen friends

49. You are a nanny to a four-year-old child who is in hospital. You have to leave him for an hour. You should:

(a) tell him you'll soon be back and leave your handbag with him
(b) wait until he is asleep and slip out
(c) tell him to be good or you won't come back
(d) pretend you are only going to the toilet

50. A child in your care has recently acquired a 'ready-made' family of siblings, through her mother's second marriage. She feels ambivalent towards these children. This means that:

(a) she is strongly resentful of their new position
(b) she is spiteful towards them
(c) she feels mixed emotions of pleasure and resentment
(d) she is delighted to have new siblings

51. A nursery school child's parents have split up recently. The father has access to his child one Sunday a month. Staff know that the mother is still feeling angry and rejected. On the day following the first access Sunday, what would be the best attitude for them to take?

   (a) Ask the mother how it went and point out what a good experience it was for the child.
   (b) Ask the child how he enjoyed his time with Daddy.
   (c) Tell the child not to talk about it because of upsetting Mummy.
   (d) Act normally and be prepared for temporary difficulties in the child's behaviour.

52. A nursery officer in day nursery finds herself unable to like a particular child. Despite giving it time, her feelings do not change. She would be advised to:

   (a) tell his parents how she feels and see what they suggest
   (b) pretend to make a favourite of him, to compensate for her feelings
   (c) say nothing to anyone and try to hide her feelings
   (d) discuss it with her officer-in-charge, with a view to his moving groups

53. A four-year-old girl gets 'stuck' at the top of a climbing frame and screams for help. The nursery nurse should:

   (a) leave her to get down alone
   (b) go up and carry her down
   (c) stand near and 'talk' her down
   (d) shout at her to get down at once

54. On holiday a three-year-old shows great fear of the sea. How can the adult help him ovecome this fear?

   (a) Carry him into the sea despite protests.
   (b) Find a rock pool for him to play in.
   (c) Tease him good humouredly.
   (d) Tell him not to be such a baby.

55. A two-year-old refuses to sit on her potty. The best way to deal with this is to:

   (a) forget about toilet training for two to three weeks
   (b) force her to sit on her potty every hour
   (c) offer her a reward for sitting on her potty
   (d) make it a game to sit on the potty

56. As an adult working in a multi-culture infant school, what should you do about the celebration of Christmas?

(a) Pretend that it is not happening.
(b) Concentrate only on Santa Claus, snow, etc.
(c) Present it as one of the religious festivals that Christians participate in.
(d) Give it great significance and hope you will not offend anyone.

57. For which activity is it least appropriate to involve parental help in infant schools?

(a) jumble sales
(b) teaching of reading
(c) cookery
(d) woodwork

58. A child who is experiencing sexual abuse within the family is likely, at nursery school, to be:

(a) withdrawn and quiet
(b) outgoing and happy
(c) interested in sexual play
(d) talkative about her experiences

59. A child will eat only fish on Friday. It could be assumed that:

(a) she does not like fish very much
(b) her family are practising Catholics
(c) she is on a special diet
(d) she and her family are Muslim

60. Which of the following terms is NOT acceptable when describing a person with a disability?

(a) a mongol
(b) a person with Down's Syndrome
(c) a person with a handicap
(d) a person who has cerebral palsy

61. The main reason for a boy to be circumcised today would be:

(a) religious
(b) medical
(c) hygiene
(d) social

44

62. A case conference is a conference about:

   (a) misbehaviour at school
   (b) an abused child
   (c) travelling with children
   (d) cases of infectious diseases

63. A key worker is:

   (a) a person who has a key to a child's home
   (b) a case coordinator in a child abuse case
   (c) a social worker in a key position
   (d) a worker in a lock factory

64. What is the 'guardian ad litem'?

   (a) a light newspaper
   (b) a person acting for the parents
   (c) a person to care for a child's interests in court
   (d) a person who is fostering a child

65. A child minder must be registered if she:

   (a) looks after a neighbour's child for an afternoon
   (b) baby-sits for a child in his own home regularly
   (c) looks after a child daily in her own home for payment
   (d) takes her one-year-old niece out for the day

66. Solvent abuse refers to:

   (a) alcoholism
   (b) drug addiction
   (c) glue sniffing
   (d) child abuse

67. The Warnock Report recommended that: 'Children with special educational needs may be placed in special schools only if their parents consent.' This statement is:

   (a) true
   (b) untrue
   (c) true in some local authorities only
   (d) true but seldom put into practice

68. Free medicines are provided in Britain to one of the following groups of people. Which is it?

   (a) all young people under eighteen
   (b) all people over sixty
   (c) all mothers of children under one year
   (d) all employees of the Health Service

69. SDA is the recognised abbreviation for:

    (a) Severe Disablement Allowance
    (b) Sudden Death Action
    (c) School Drama Association
    (d) Social Diseases Anonymous

70. 'In loco parentis' means:

    (a) a train outing for parents
    (b) in place of parents
    (c) Latin motto for train drivers
    (d) Latin name for a virus

71. Which one of the following services is the responsibility of the Environmental Health Department?

    (a) Notification of Infectious Diseases
    (b) Inspection of Accident Books
    (c) Repair of drains and sewers
    (d) Monitoring of Noise Abatement

72. In which of the following areas do the Citizens Advice Bureaux provide information?

    (a) medical advice
    (b) housing advice
    (c) travel advice
    (d) tourism data

73. A school crossing patrol person can legally stop traffic provided:

    (a) she is helping children to cross the road
    (b) she is dressed in state-approved uniform
    (c) she is known by head teachers to be reliable
    (d) she is sufficiently tall to be seen

74. The parents of a nanny's 'charge' come home from work tired and irritable. Their three-year-old has been particularly obstructive that day. Should the nanny:

    (a) tell them about the misdeeds straight away to get it over with
    (b) make no reference at all to his behaviour
    (c) await a suitable moment, then make gentle reference to it
    (d) make the child tell the parents at once about his misdeeds

75. A student, outside placement, discovers something about a child's background which throws considerable light on her behaviour at nursery, and special allowances needing to be made. She should:

   (a) keep quiet, as it is none of her business
   (b) ask the child kindly if what she has heard is true
   (c) tell her closest friend and ask for advice
   (d) speak confidentially to the officer-in-charge

76. A non-English speaking mother brings a half-filled bottle of antibiotic medicine to nursery for her child. It appears to be two to three weeks' old. What steps should the nursery officer take to obtain correct information?

   (a) Ask the mother about the medicine by sign language.
   (b) Ask the sibling who speaks English.
   (c) Contact the child's social worker.
   (d) Contact the child's health visitor.

77. BAECE is the abbreviated name for:

   (a) a make of construction toys for children
   (b) the British Association for Education (Church of England)
   (c) the British Association for Early Childhood Education
   (d) British/American Early Childhood Education

78. The main aim of the National Childbirth Trust is:

   (a) education for parenthood
   (b) natural childbirth for everyone
   (c) registration of all births
   (d) home confinement for all mothers

79. A contract for a nanny working in a private family is essential because it will:

   (a) make it easier for her to leave
   (b) explain how to perform her duties
   (c) define the terms of employment
   (d) ensure she has a room of her own

80. The chief aim of nanny-contact clubs is to:

   (a) encourage nannies to form a union
   (b) introduce local nannies to one another
   (c) introduce nannies to boyfriends
   (d) form a babysitting circle

EXAMPLE 2 OF AN ESSAY PAPER

You will have three hours for the whole paper, and must answer one question from each of Sections A, B, C and D. The maximum marks for these are shown in the right hand column

SECTION A

Marks

A1 Describe the stages of weaning in a child's first year.   **7**
Give a typical day's diet for a one-year-old.   **3**

or

A2 How could you help a child with one of the following conditions to integrate into a nursery class?
(a) partial hearing
(b) speech defect
(c) partial sight   **6**
What are the benefits to all concerned of such an integration?   **4**

SECTION B

B1 Modern technology has an increasingly important place in today's infant classrooms.
Using your own experience, describe how one such piece of equipment can contribute to children's all-round development.   **7**
Have you encountered any problems associated with it?   **3**

or

B2 How can young children gain from contact with adults at nursery school/class?   **6**
How can staff extend this contact to include adults in the outside world?   **4**

48

SECTION C

C1 Children are often placed in a day nursery because they are 'at risk'. What does this mean?   **2**
What are the special responsibilities of the nursery officer to such a child in her family group?   **5**
Outline the procedure if the child arrives at nursery with an injury.   **3**

or

C2 What effect could a father's unemployment have on a family with small children?   **7**
What services are available to help this family?   **3**

SECTION D

D1 Before opening your own private day nursery, what factors would you need to consider and explore?   **6**
What outside agencies would be involved?   **4**

or

D2 You have applied for a post as nanny to a young family in London.
How would you prepare for the interview?   **5**
What subjects would need to be discussed?   **5**

Here is one way in which a good candidate might answer Sections A, B, C and D.

SECTION A

A1: Plan

WEANING STAGES   Savoury taste – semi-liquid.
Three tastes a day.
Increase and vary.
Increase 'dinner'.
Replace bottle with drink in cup.
Replace early morning milk with water.
Bring mealtimes in line with family.
Change to more solid texture.
Finger food.
Change to cow's milk.

DAY'S DIET TO	Protein – egg, meat, fish, cheese
INCLUDE	Iron – egg, meat
	Vitamin A, D, – milk one pint daily
	Vitamin C – fruit, vegetables
	Vitamin B – Marmite, brown bread

Contrast texture and colour

Essay

By the time a baby reaches three to four months of age, she is ready to begin the gradual change-over from milk to mixed diet. Usually she will show that she is ready for weaning because extra milk will not satisfy her hunger. Even if this does not happen, it will be necessary from about four months of age to introduce food such as meat and eggs which contain iron. This is because milk contains very little iron, and the baby's store obtained before birth needs to be replenished.

A baby should be introduced to savoury-tasting food first, in order to educate her taste. If sugar or sugary foods are given too early, a baby may become addicted and refuse to eat non-sweet foods.

By about three months of age most babies are settled into a fairly regular feeding, either having breast milk or powdered baby milk five times a day – roughly 6 a.m., 10 a.m., 2 p.m., 6 p.m. and 10 p.m. Weaning begins by introducing the baby to 'tastes' of different foods in semi-liquid form before the 10 a.m., 2 p.m. and 6 p.m. milk feed. The first 'taste' can be given before the 2 p.m. feed and this will eventually become her dinner or lunch. The easiest food to use at this stage is one of the savoury powdered baby foods made especially for weaning babies. The powder is mixed with boiled water in a cup and given to the baby in a plastic spoon. The baby should be supported in a sitting position on her mother's knee and the 'taste' should be followed by the breast or bottle feed.

Some early difficulties may be experienced. She may spit out this first taste. However, with perseverance she will usually take a teaspoonful, although sometimes it will be necessary to give her some of her milk first.

Two to three days after the successful acceptance of the 'dinner', another 'taste' can be introduced at the 6 p.m. feed – this time a teaspoonful of mashed ripe banana or some liquidised stewed apple, followed by the usual breast or bottle milk. Two days later the third 'taste' can be introduced at the 10 a.m. feed – a teaspoonful of 'baby rice' mixed with milk.

Once these three tastes have been established it will be necessary to increase and vary the meals, never introducing more than one new food a day in case she is upset by it. Most people concentrate on increasing the 2 p.m. feed, introducing home-cooked meat and vegetables and gravy which have been liquidised. Gradually, as the baby eats more food, she will take less and less milk. When this happens, water or very dilute fruit juice can be offered in a small cup instead of the milk. At this stage she will probably want her 6 p.m. feed earlier, in which case her meals can be moved into line with the family times. If she is given water instead of milk when she wakes in the morning, she will be ready for her breakfast at 8 a.m., so that lunch can be moved back to 12 midday, tea at 4 p.m. and finally milk at bedtime, 7–8 p.m. Foods such as egg yolk, egg custard, steamed fish, liver, kidney, grated cheese or cereal, and vegetables can be introduced gradually.

From five to six months of age, when the baby starts chewing, she should be given mashed, rather than liquidised, food. After six months of age fresh cow's milk can be given in place of powdered baby milk. When the baby appears to be ready, the tea-time bottle may be replaced with a cup of milk or milky tea and, later, the breakfast bottle also. Most babies need to retain the bedtime bottle until at least one year of age because they gain comfort from sucking, as well as needing the milk.

When the baby is able to sit for short periods in a high chair with a tray and begins to put things into her mouth accurately (about six to seven months) she can be given 'finger' food, starting with a hard rusk to chew, thus helping her jaw development and teething.

As she grows bigger, a wider variety of food may be given. At breakfast time she can have adult cereals such as 'Weetabix' or porridge, followed by scrambled or boiled egg and toast fingers if wanted. Small sandwiches using brown bread and containing tomato flesh, grated cheese or chopped hard-boiled egg can be given at tea-time, together with plain sponge cake. As soon as she shows interest she should be encouraged to try and feed herself. Lunch food should be chopped, rather than mashed, so that the baby can pick it up with her fingers. A spoon should be supplied and her mother or nurse can 'help' spoonfeed her at the same time. She should be allowed to experiment and try to feed herself. Usually babies will copy other members of their families if they sit with them at mealtimes and, when hungry, can be very efficient at feeding themselves by the age of one year.

A typical diet for a one-year-old may be as follows:

On waking: Water or diluted
                unsweetened fruit juice

Breakfast: Weetabix and milk   Milk to drink
                Toast and Marmite

Lunch:	Minced meat	Carrots
	Mashed potato	Pieces of orange
	Chopped cabbage	Water to drink
Tea:	Scrambled egg and	Piece of sponge cake
	tomato	Banana
	Brown bread and butter	
Bedtime:	Milk or hot chocolate	

A2: Plan

(a) PARTIAL HEARING

Help integration
1. Explain to other children.
2. Show him around.
3. Let mother stay with him.
4. Make sure he sits where he can see and hear.
5. Talk to him and make sure he can see you talk.
6. Look after his hearing aid.

Benefits
For child:
   Hears normal speech.
   Plays with normal children.
   Better able to cope with infant school.

Other children:
   Will begin to understand about handicaps.
   Will accept children with handicaps more naturally.

Mother:
   Feels supported.
   Has some respite from coping with child.

(b) SPEECH DEFECT
As above except 6

As above

(c) PARTIAL SIGHT
As above except 6

As above

52

SECTION B

B1: Plan

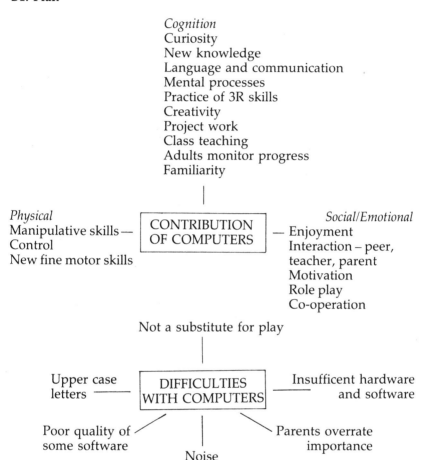

Cognition
Curiosity
New knowledge
Language and communication
Mental processes
Practice of 3R skills
Creativity
Project work
Class teaching
Adults monitor progress
Familiarity

Physical
Manipulative skills —
Control
New fine motor skills

CONTRIBUTION OF COMPUTERS

Social/Emotional
— Enjoyment
Interaction – peer,
teacher, parent
Motivation
Role play
Co-operation

Not a substitute for play

Upper case letters ——

DIFFICULTIES WITH COMPUTERS

—— Insufficent hardware and software

Poor quality of some software

Noise

Parents overrate importance

Essay

Computers are commonly found in infant schools today, and even very young children are familiar with them. All the children I have watched operating have been thoroughly enjoying themselves. Children seldom seem to quarrel over turn-taking, and you often hear them planning together.

There is much opportunity for adult/child interaction, with parents as well as teachers and staff. One unemployed father was a great help in his twice-weekly sessions with 'middle infants'.

53

Children get immediate feedback if they make a mistake on a program, so do not have the discouraging sight of crosses on exercise books, or correction by teachers. They do not have to waste time queuing at the teacher's desk for help. 'Rewards' are often amusing, so motivation is good. Successful completion of puzzles, etc. for abler children brings a real sense of achievement. There is a certain amount of role play involved when children have to project into very different characters, like beings from outer space.

Using the keyboard and co-ordinating finger movements promotes manipulative skill and control. Some manual skills, like dressing, for example, can be taught and practised through computer programs, with the youngest infants.

Not surprisingly, the main contribution that computers make is in cognitive development. Children's curiosity is also harnessed, and they can discover new factual information – about nature, for example.

A great deal of language is involved; children use it to describe, predict, dictate direction – 'further up', 'to the right', 'too far' and so on.

Children have to listen carefully, intepret symbols and meanings. They need to think logically, make decisions, predict outcomes, remember, estimate, sequence correctly, and solve problems. They also need to concentrate very hard. Computers provide a lively way of practising what could be boring 3R skills in matching, rules of number, spelling, word order, and so on.

Content-free software enables children, with the help of a sufficiently interested adult, to make their own banks of information. This may be about topic work, or data about themselves – height, weight, shoe size, etc. They can then do simple statistical analysis on this.

Further possibilities exist, and word processors can, for instance, offer an alternative approach to creative writing. Computer activities can form part of a class project, for example on frogs. Occasionally, more difficult concepts, such as symmetry or direction, can be taught to a whole group, so that the computer takes the place of the old-fashioned blackboard.

Skilled adults will be able to assess from watching the speed and ease with which children carry out their activities when and how they are ready to progress. Getting used to keyboards and micro-computer technology generally must stand children in good stead for later schooling, and adult life.

Problems met in using computers in the classroom are, I believe, largely problems of management. If there is only one computer in a school, each class does not get enough experience with it for the children to get past the novelty-reaction stage. It is also difficult for the teacher to integrate the computer fully into the learning programmes (curriculum), and for all to see it as yet another aid to learning. Sometimes parents get anxious about how much access *their* child has to it. Some parents even judge a school by how much hardware and software it possesses.

Upper-case letters on a keyboard could pose problems to children learning to read and write predominantly in lower-case letters. This, however, can be overcome by sticky labels, or by supplying the concept keyboard for young children.

Not all software is of excellent quality; some programs offer repetitive practice in certain skills, and the themes of others are based on aggressiveness. Some programs give a more amusing response to a wrong tactic, for example, blowing a 'raspberry', than the response to the correct tactic. The noises produced can be irritating and intrusive to others in, or near, the room, who are not themselves participating.

A disproportionate amount of time spent sitting in front of a VDU might not only tire children's eyes, but it is also too static an occupation for young children. Nothing can replace children's all-important vigorous physical play and the development of their gross and fine motor skills. But, used wisely, computers can bring about a most beneficial widening of children's experience.

B2: Plan

(a) *Benefit to children*
   Children will receive and see a model of good child care practice.
   Individual attention and more time.
   Skilled and expert handling (e.g. of behaviour problems).
   Provision of stimulating play materials and stimulation of other kinds.
   Sustained conversation and new ways of communicating.
   Gradual weaning from parent.
   Encouragement to independence.
   Different hobbies and interests.
   'Opposite' sex adult for single-parent family children.
   Builds confidence.
   Knowledge that everyone has a contribution to make, e.g. 'Lollipop lady'.

(b) *Extending contact with the outside world*
   Bring in police officer, fire officer, Road Safety Officers.
   Bring in parents with special skills, e.g. instrumental, or interests
   – cooking.
   Bring in parents who do interesting jobs, e.g. farmer.
   Bring in fathers, to benefit children of single-parent families.
   Encourage links with community, special schools, playgroup, local churches.

Bring in parents from various ethnic groups.
Encourage these to share cultural patterns, e.g. cooking.
Co-operate with mother-tongue work.
Bring in specialists offering help for children with physical difficulties (speech therapist), learning or behaviour problems (Child and Family Guidance Service).
Encourage health education, e.g. through school nurse, dentist.
Include parents on many school activities (swimming?) and outings. Encourage links with other age groups, e.g. secondary school children, grandparents.
Take children out:

    on local, impromptu visits, e.g. road repairs
    on organised trips, e.g. zoo, wildlife park
    to local library
    to local shops for cooking requirements
    to fire station, other local services
    on different forms of transport

SECTION C

C1: Plan

AT RISK	Likely to be abused (Note: only two marks. Be brief.)
RESPONSIBILITY	Key worker
	Keep records
	Height and weight
	Medical
	Observation – check on bruises
	Discretion
	Involve parents
PROCEDURE	'Red' book in Avon
	Explanation
	Chief nursery officer
	Key worker or case co-ordinator
	Local authority medical officer
	Hospital
	Place of safety
	Case conference
	Health visitor
	Record – date, time

Essay

Children are said to be 'at risk' when there is reason to believe they may be abused by their parents or guardian or other relatives. Usually there will be a history of past minor injuries or 'accidents', or the parents may be having difficulty in providing adequate care, owing to factors such as low intelligence, mental illness or ignorance. There may also be associated social problems such as unemployment. When a child is found to be in such a situation, a case conference should be convened so that all the workers involved with the family can get together and exchange information, discuss their fears and come to a group decision on a plan of action to help both the child and the family. The child's name will be placed on an 'At Risk' register and a 'key' worker will be appointed to co-ordinate all the work with the family. Part of this plan of action could be the admission of the child to a day nursery.

When an 'at risk' child is admitted to a nursery, it is very important to ensure that all his details are recorded correctly. In addition, the name, address and telephone of his key worker, his doctor and his health visitor should be noted. All members of the nursery staff will therefore know whom to contact should there be any problems or queries. For instance, if the child is absent at any time, the key worker should be informed so that she can decide whether a visit to the family should be made to ensure the safety of the child.

Usually, on a child's entry to a nursery, a medical examination is arranged so that his physical condition can be ascertained, and any health problems can be dealt with. At the same time his height and weight will be recorded and these physical details should be monitored throughout the child's stay in the nursery, as they are a good indication of the child's state of health.

The child should be examined each day for any signs of injury, but this should be done discreetly and tactfully, so that the child is not made aware of being treated differently. Any bruises or other marks must be noted on his records and his mother or guardian should be asked in a matter-of-fact way for an explanation of any injury. The head of the nursery should also be informed of any injury.

It is important for the nursery officer to behave in a professional manner when dealing with such a child and to be careful to avoid implying any criticism of the child's parents, because – even if such criticism is true – it will not be helpful either to the child or his parents.

The general care of this child will be the same as for any other child, but the provision for his physical, emotional and mental needs is very important. This child may need more reassurance and more demonstrations of affection if he is not to feel to blame for his parents' actions. He will need to be assured that he is a worthwhile person and that the treatment he has received was not something he deserved. His self-esteem can be bolstered by good care from his nursery officer, and this will stand him in good stead in the future. His parents may also need special help, and it may be desirable for them to become involved in the child's care at nursery so that they can learn by example. The aim would be to try to help the parents to become better parents and, again, a non-critical attitude from the nursery officer is vital.

In most areas there are guidelines describing the correct procedure to follow if a child is found to have been injured. In Avon,* the 'red' book, which is issued to all day nurseries, etc., lays down the following procedure:

1. Ask for an explanation of the injury.
   Does the explanation seem valid?

2. Inform the chief nursery officer, who should:
   (a) contact the key worker
   (b) either ask the local medical officer to examine the child or take him to a hospital casualty department for examination and treatment
   (c) ensure that the child remains in a place of safety until a case conference can be arranged
   (d) inform the child's health visitor.

3. Write a full statement as soon as you can, while the incident is fresh in your mind. Sign it and add the date and time when it was written.

C2: Plan

UNEMPLOYMENT *Disadvantages*
EFFECT   Lower standard of living:
      food
      clothing
      holidays
      home-heating
Poor health caused by poor nutrition
Housing problems – if paying mortgage
Mental problems because of stress
Father:
      depressed, suicidal tendencies, child abuse
      frustrated
      loss of prestige
Mother:
      may have to work
      strain of parents being together all the time
      marital problems

*Use the procedure current in the area in which *you* work, which may differ from this.

Advantages
Father:
    more time with children
    may bring parents closer together
    may have redundancy pay

HELP

Unemployment pay
Redundancy pay
Retraining programmes – Job Centres
Social Security
Social Services – social worker
Marriage Guidance
Legal aid
Day nursery/child care
Health Service
NSPCC
CAB

SECTION D

D1: Plan

Essay

When planning to start a nursery there are so many factors to consider that it is difficult to decide what to do first. However, I would need to have had several years' experience, both in working with children and in administration, in order to convince a bank or some other institution that the proposal could succeed, and that it would be worth advancing money to help finance it. It would also be a great help to have money of my own to put in. I think I would try to find a colleague to go into partnership in order to share the responsibility and cost and to provide some of the expertise. It would be a good idea for one of us to take a 'small business course', as run by the Manpower Services Commission, to learn the basis of book-keeping, cash flow and the general administration of a business.

Perhaps the next step would be to decide the best position for a nursery (unless there was an existing one available to buy). A large-scale map of the city area where I wished to work could be marked with all the public and private nursery facilities. This would help pinpoint any gaps. Looking at these districts selectively, I could narrow down the areas to those where a nursery would be needed. For instance, a position close to a housing estate which has been established between three and ten years would be ideal because there should be many families with children of nursery age. Several visits would be made to likely areas, to make a note of the local facilities and look for either a suitable building for conversion or a building site within 'pram-pushing' distance of potential clients.

At this stage it would be worth making contact with the teachers at the local primary school and the health visitors at the local health centre, as they can provide a lot of the information needed. I would need to know when the children in the area usually start school, as this can vary from starting in the term they are five years of age to starting at the beginning of the academic year in which they are five years old. If the former is the case, then there will be a fairly urgent need for provision for the four-to-five-year-old children who are bored at home. If the latter is the case, then it will be necessary to concentrate on the two-to-four-year-olds.

It will also be necessary to know something about the families living in the area. For instance, do most of the women work? And are they mostly families of one to two children where the child will need the companionship of other children? A decision will have to be made about the age group to cater for, as the regulations differ for each group. Most nurseries only take children from two to five years because children under two years need so much more concentrated attention than the older ones.

Estate agents should be approached for information about suitable accommodation, and a solicitor and, possibly, an accountant may be needed to cope with the negotiations. Once a building is chosen, planning permission must be obtained to enable it to be used as a nursery. A mortgage will be needed and also money for equipment and the initial running costs.

The Social Services Department must be informed of the intention to open a nursery, as the premises must be inspected and approved for registration. Rules are laid down concerning the ratio of children to adults, the toilet facilities, the outdoor play areas and so on, and these rules must be observed. Both the Fire Department and the Environmental Health Department will have to be informed and both will inspect the building.

Once the numbers and ages of the children are estimated, the number of staff can be calculated and advertising and interviewing can begin. Furniture and equipment can be selected, decorations chosen and indoor and outdoor play areas planned. Decisions can be made about hours of opening and whether children will attend full-time or part-time or a mixture of both. If children are going to stay all day, then meals will have to be provided – this will entail the provision of good kitchen accommodation and a dining area, and the staff will have to include a cook and kitchen helper(s).

Insurance, both of the building and to cover the children and employees, must be arranged. Advertising should begin early, in order to create a waiting list so that there will be sufficient children to start on opening day, to make the business viable. Charges to the parents will have to be decided in advance, and for this the expenses of the nursery will have to be calculated carefully to obtain a balance and make the nursery able to pay its way.

Starting a nursery from scratch would be extremely hard work but I am sure it would be well worth while to myself and the parents and children it will serve.

D2: Plan

(a) *Preparing for the interview*
Plan clothes and appearance, journey, timing, etc.
Prepare necessities (certificate, money, C.V., spare tights, etc.)
Think out possible questions and answers
Think out questions to ask
Investigate area beforehand (i.e. for social life, nanny contact) and cost of travel home.

(b) *Subjects to be discussed*
Details of family and children
Definition of role and responsibilities

Contract – conditions of service, etc.
Pay
Payment of income tax and National Insurance
Free time, weekends off, etc.
Accommodation
Parents' expectations
Other help in home
Holidays
Minimum period of employment/trial period

J. Robertson

MULTIPLE CHOICE PAPER
EXAMPLE 1: CORRECT ANSWERS

The answers are shown in a form which resembles the grid method used in the actual examination. In each case the *correct* answer is indicated by an underline.

1 a b <u>c</u> d	28 <u>a</u> b c d	55 <u>a</u> b c d
2 a <u>b</u> c d	29 a b c <u>d</u>	56 a b <u>c</u> d
3 a b <u>c</u> d	30 <u>a</u> b c d	57 a <u>b</u> c d
4 <u>a</u> b c d	31 a b <u>c</u> d	58 a b c <u>d</u>
5 a b <u>c</u> d	32 a b <u>c</u> d	59 <u>a</u> b c d
6 a <u>b</u> c d	33 a b <u>c</u> d	60 a <u>b</u> c d
7 a b <u>c</u> d	34 a <u>b</u> c d	61 a <u>b</u> c d
8 <u>a</u> b c d	35 <u>a</u> b c d	62 <u>a</u> b c d
9 a b c <u>d</u>	36 a <u>b</u> c d	63 <u>a</u> b c d
10 a <u>b</u> c d	37 a <u>b</u> c d	64 a b <u>c</u> d
11 <u>a</u> b c d	38 a b <u>c</u> d	65 <u>a</u> b c d
12 a <u>b</u> c d	39 a b <u>c</u> d	66 a <u>b</u> c d
13 a b c <u>d</u>	40 a <u>b</u> c d	67 a b <u>c</u> d
14 a <u>b</u> c d	41 a b c <u>d</u>	68 a <u>b</u> c d
15 <u>a</u> b c d	42 a b <u>c</u> d	69 a <u>b</u> c d
16 a b <u>c</u> d	43 a <u>b</u> c d	70 a b <u>c</u> d
17 <u>a</u> b c d	44 <u>a</u> b c d	71 <u>a</u> b c d
18 a b c <u>d</u>	45 a b <u>c</u> d	72 a b <u>c</u> d
19 a <u>b</u> c d	46 a <u>b</u> c d	73 a b c <u>d</u>
20 a <u>b</u> c d	47 <u>a</u> b c d	74 a <u>b</u> c d
21 a <u>b</u> c d	48 <u>a</u> b c d	75 a b <u>c</u> d
22 a b <u>c</u> d	49 a b <u>c</u> d	76 a b c <u>d</u>
23 a b c <u>d</u>	50 a <u>b</u> c d	77 <u>a</u> b c d
24 <u>a</u> b c d	51 a b c <u>d</u>	78 a b <u>c</u> d
25 a <u>b</u> c d	52 <u>a</u> b c d	79 a <u>b</u> c d
26 a b c <u>d</u>	53 a b c <u>d</u>	80 a <u>b</u> c d
27 a b c <u>d</u>	54 a <u>b</u> c d	

MULTIPLE CHOICE PAPER
EXAMPLE 2: CORRECT ANSWERS

1	a b <u>c</u> d	28	a b <u>c</u> d	55	<u>a</u> b c d
2	a b <u>c</u> d	29	<u>a</u> b c d	56	a b <u>c</u> d
3	a b <u>c</u> d	30	a b <u>c</u> d	57	a <u>b</u> c d
4	<u>a</u> b c d	31	a b c <u>d</u>	58	<u>a</u> b c d
5	a b c <u>d</u>	32	a <u>b</u> c d	59	a <u>b</u> c d
6	a b c <u>d</u>	33	a <u>b</u> c d	60	<u>a</u> b c d
7	a <u>b</u> c d	34	a b <u>c</u> d	61	<u>a</u> b c d
8	<u>a</u> b c d	35	a <u>b</u> c d	62	a <u>b</u> c d
9	a b c <u>d</u>	36	a <u>b</u> c d	63	a <u>b</u> c d
10	a b <u>c</u> d	37	a b c <u>d</u>	64	a b <u>c</u> d
11	a b c <u>d</u>	38	a b <u>c</u> d	65	a b <u>c</u> d
12	a b <u>c</u> d	39	<u>a</u> b c d	66	a b <u>c</u> d
13	a <u>b</u> c d	40	a b c <u>d</u>	67	<u>a</u> b c d
14	a b <u>c</u> d	41	a b c <u>d</u>	68	a b <u>c</u> d
15	a <u>b</u> c d	42	<u>a</u> b c d	69	<u>a</u> b c d
16	a <u>b</u> c d	43	a <u>b</u> c d	70	a <u>b</u> c d
17	<u>a</u> b c d	44	a b c <u>d</u>	71	a b c <u>d</u>
18	a <u>b</u> c d	45	a b <u>c</u> d	72	a <u>b</u> c d
19	<u>a</u> b c d	46	a b c <u>d</u>	73	a <u>b</u> c d
20	a <u>b</u> c d	47	a b c <u>d</u>	74	a b <u>c</u> d
21	a <u>b</u> c d	48	a b c <u>d</u>	75	a b c <u>d</u>
22	<u>a</u> b c d	49	<u>a</u> b c d	76	a b c <u>d</u>
23	<u>a</u> b c d	50	a b <u>c</u> d	77	a b <u>c</u> d
24	a <u>b</u> c d	51	a b c <u>d</u>	78	<u>a</u> b c d
25	a b c <u>d</u>	52	a b c <u>d</u>	79	a b <u>c</u> d
26	a b c <u>d</u>	53	a b <u>c</u> d	80	a <u>b</u> c d
27	a b <u>c</u> d	54	a <u>b</u> c d		